Sensational Spectacular

Nate Pritts

BlazeVOX [books]

Buffalo, New York

Sensational Spectacular by Nate Pritts
Copyright © 2007

Published by BlazeVOX [books]

Printed in the United States of America

Front cover art, "Empathy and Texture in Blue,"
by Rhonda Gleason-Pritts

Back cover wood photo by Hedda Gjerpen

Cover design by Scott O'Connor for GO Studios
[gostudiosla.com]

Book design by Geoffrey Gatza
First Edition

ISBN: 1-934289-06-X   ISBN 13: 978-1-
934289-06-8
Library of Congress Control Number: 2006938621

BlazeVOX [books]
14 Tremaine Ave
Kenmore, NY 14217
Editor@blazevox.org

publisher of weird little books

BlazeVOX [books]

blazevox.org

2   4   6   8   0   9   7   5   3   1

B   X

Acknowledgements—

Thanks to the editors & readers of the following journals, print & online, where some of these poems first appeared, often in earlier forms:

88, Alice Blue, The Bedazzler, Cab/Net, Coconut, Concelebratory Shoehorn Review, Copper Nickel, DIAGRAM, 42Opus, Greensboro Review, Gulf Coast, Keepgoing, No Tell Motel, Past Simple, RealPoetik, Segue, StorySouth & TKO

Several of the poems in the second section were included in my chapbook *Big Crisis* (Forklift, Ink). Thanks go out to Eric Appleby & Matt Hart for making that happen.

Thanks for sensational help & support & friendship to Matt Dube, Matt Hart (again!), & Scott O'Connor, whose separate enthusiasms for this project always matched & often outstripped my own. Also, to three friends from back home, years ago: Brian, Carlo, & Paolo.

Thanks are due to Mike Voiles, for access to his amazing world, & to Geoffrey Gatza for his energy & dedication.

Final & most spectacular thanks to my family—Kate, Dylan, Laney & O, M & A—but most of all to my wife Rhonda for being with me through everything for ever.

Table of Contents

1: SECRET ORIGINS   11

2: BIG CRISIS   27

    In Pieces   29
    The Moon's Invisible Army   31
    Isle of No Return   32
    The Fastest Man Alive   33
    Love Song from the Dawn of Time   34
    Living Whirlpool   35
    Creatures from the Past   36
    Great Thunder!   37
    Without A Net   38
    Sun Brain   39
    Human Pets   40
    Space-Boomerang Trap   41
    Poof   42
    Loss Time   43
    Horrible Dreams   44
    Tomorrow Beast   46
    The Walls of Our Sphere   47
    Never Be The Same Again   48
    Duel on the Island   49
    A Day in the Life   50
    Thousand-Year Separation   51
    Requiem for the End of Time!   52
    In the Hot Seat   53

3: THE BRAVE & THE BOLD   57

Sensational Spectacular

1: SECRET ORIGINS

I never mentioned my friends in my poems [...]

Although they meant almost more than
anything to me
Of this now for some time I've felt
an attenuation
So I'm mentioning them maybe this will
bring them back to me

—Kenneth Koch, "Circus II"

:World of No Return!:

My friends & I, we've got it all
figured out. We play a game

where we sit facing each other, stone-
faced, unblinking &, after one wrong move,

we watch a staticy purple light engulf
that one poor one who won't come back no more.

:Those Ghost Hands Reaching:

Each of us has a job: pull, push, ram

headlong. Not one of us alone could hope to keep
the shiny gold door closed by their lonesome self!
Way up above anyone's head we see it

swinging open, those two chalk-colored hands
reaching through. It's easy to assume hostile intent.
What good has ever come from ghost hands

reaching through a floating gold door?

:Space Ship:

Miles above the Earth, in our long yellow boat,
my friends & I get all weepy

about the many burger joints we can't visit back home
since we are, as I said, miles above the Earth.
"There was one that would not allow the use of ketchup,"
said my friend in green, the earnest one.
"One demanded the addition of pickles,"
said my friend in red who is always joking
in a way that makes everyone feel vague & colorless.

Space stretched out before us, infinite. My stomach
grumbled, aching for destination.

:The Story You've Been Waiting For:

My friends & I believe in excluding newcomers

from our secrets: secret lair, secret handshake.

We collect our separate feelings of scorn

& rage & elitism the way other groups of friends

collect sea shells on the shore of the vast

ocean of *Hello!* But we are protected, encased

in a diamond-hard sense of self worth. Shoot

arrows at us & see if you can break through.

Secretly, it's what we most want.

:Gravity Gone Wild:

Normally rooted, feet stuck to the pavement,
we've recently lost our footing. I speak for all of us
in my big collective voice that repeats the important words:
rooted, stuck, lost, all, voice. Repeat.

Now I see into each window on the highest floors
of the city buildings that usually loom over me.
People are in there, rugs, lamps & magazines. People.
Floating away, my brain unclenches. Repeat.

:The Wheel of Misfortune:

I am my own jackpot, the square you hope

to land on, & I am my own best friend,

I date my girlfriend & claim it was a misunderstanding.

I am the trip to Antigua that you'll never take,

& I am the cruise line your neighbors swear by

that makes you feel your life is small. I am

slowly spinning out of control.

:Funhouse Mirror:

Hidden behind the mirror, from my heartbreakingly
secure perspective, I tell my friends the truth:

"Those outfits you're wearing look ridiculous,"
I say over my right shoulder, left hand on the doorknob,

feet jittery but ready. The truth
makes me want to run for the screaming hills.

:For Sale:

Men with hats are taking bids on my friends.

The availability of my friend in green, the earnest one,
initiates a bidding war among only the bidders with hats *& mustaches*.

My friend in red, whose jokes fall flat, sold quickly
but for much less than was polite. Slowly, the men with hats

buy up all my friends & I'm left alone on stage
with no idea how to gauge my worth.

:That Time of Year:

One Saturday morning, my friend in blue says
we should all pretend to be trees.

Immediately I can feel my fingers getting brittle, my arms stiff.

My other friends & I start to grumble in low, guttural
tree-talk. "Just wait," says my friend in blue

whose vast stores of patience have sent
his anger into long hibernation. "Just wait
until your hands grow buds & those buds bloom."

:The Enemy:

My friends & I, we have only one real enemy
but he is a flake & so we don't worry about him much.
Sometimes he'll see us walking around the mall together

& he'll come running over, his big dumb mouth opening wide.
It is hard for us to look at him; he wears a silly headband
with pictures of the moons & stars. They don't glow

the way the real moon & stars would. Red
always tries to say something to lighten the mood:
"Is that a moon on your head or is the angle of descent

really just a luminous good time?" Our enemy holds up both hands,
all ten fingers spread out, & talks & talks until we are late
for the movie we were hoping to see. This is, usually,

the extent of his villainy. But once he smiled
when I stubbed my toe. His intentions clear, his inner evil
showing, my friends & I have tried to avoid him ever since.

:One-Hour Conquest, No Waiting:

A few of my friends have trapped themselves
from time to time. In a swirl of green smoke
meant to symbolize their flagging powers

& diminishing size, they get sucked up
inside & put on the shelf. It seems the more
friends get trapped, the easier it is to trap the rest.

My plan is to paint my skin pink & sing loud songs.
Maybe then the clock will tick by
without boredom working against me.

:Journey to the Stars:

My friends & I visit the planetarium on two-for-one day.

My earnest friend in green stares at the light bulb light of stars
& planets as if he is intimately familiar with the architecture
of space. My friend in red spends his time trying to stifle

obvious jokes. Suddenly we're all traveling through time,
seeing the sky as it will be in six months, in six thousand years.
A man tells us to keep our eyes on the skies, that we wouldn't want

to look down & see what the world around us is turning into.

:Just Us Robots!:

Someone has made robot duplicates
of my friends & I. How you can tell is that
they are all sleek metal, & naked.

These naked robot duplicates
have a different idea of fun
than the human clothed versions.

They clunk around saying things like "Bzrt."
& "Squee." My friend in red says, quietly, "Let's ditch."
One by one we get up & walk out on these misunderstood

& inarticulate versions of ourselves.

:Bowled Over:

My friends & I enjoy competitive games.
For example: bowling. For example:

bird watching. Just mention any activity
in which you could declare someone a winner

& my friends & I will line up like pins
at the end of a long slick alley. My friend

in blue tries to see only blue birds, turning a blind eye
on birds of any other color. His bird watching totals

are staggeringly low. My friend in red counts
anything he sees in the sky as a bird: airplanes,

dandelion pollen, clouds.

:The Untouchable Alien:

My friends & I, we have only one real enemy.
But we often wrestle with ourselves

over big questions & abstract concepts. Red
vibrates when he realizes that people
don't really like him. My earnest friend in green
only displays his angry side when faced with a head
bigger than his. Blue folds himself into a ball
when he thinks the universe is holding goodies
meant for him behind its inky & star-filled back.

I picture a large stone beast lumbering towards me,
heart thumping just out of reach.

:I Wish a Rocket Would Come & Take Me Away:

Sometimes when we're bored,
my friends & I twirl around
in circles as fast as we can

until we get dizzy & have to sit down.
Our dreams are dreams
of velocity & truth, of lifting
out of ourselves for a better place.

:Micro-Friends:

Lately, one of my friends has grown
to gigantic proportions. Everything
has been going his way so he swells
in physical size to keep pace
with his swelling sense of self-worth.

The rest of us scurry around his ankles
trying to get a message to him.
His vast new plain of perception
does not include us: small, hopeless,
the ones he saw shrink before his eyes.

:Traitors:

My friends & I walk a thin line between universal adulation
& scoffing disinterest. It only takes one wrong move

to turn the crowd against us. This bright morning,
picketing my house: one hundred thousand angry faces

holding up signs naming me traitor. But I never avowed belief
in any cause at all! I called my friends & the situation

was the same in each instance. Our plan was to cross
the curved crimson bridge in the small hours before dawn,

board a rocket & head to the moon. But we imagined
we'd offend the moon rocks. So we thought, collectively,

to steer clear of everything. I've committed no action,
spoken no word, in two months. My slate is almost clean.

:Mysterious Spaceman:

One day, my friends & I saw a huge man

in a space suit, plucking buildings from the ground
the same lazy way we would pick up
a dandelion & pop its head off. We thought it best

to travel different roads in the future.

:Prison House of the Morning Star:

We occasionally get into trouble, my friends & I.

There was the time my friend in red was being chased
by invisible werewolves. We built an invisible barricade
to keep the invisible werewolves out, but my friend in red
still claims to hear silent howls in the night. One other time,

my friends & I got ourselves trapped in individual-sized
prisons. We could no longer perform our secret handshake,
kept distant from each other by the unique quality of the bars.

The prisons themselves seemed to grow smaller as night
came on & then, with a blink, they were gone. We were ecstatic until,
in daylight, we realized the bars had formed snug to our bodies,

that we'd wear them always & unnoticeably.

:Carpe Diem:

My friends & I are often engaged in
deep & philosophical discussions
of the late-night variety. Our favorite concept

is something we call *outer*. Red says we
spend all our lives in *outer* while
Green says we must balance *outer* with *inner*.
Red responds by saying *typical*. All I know

is that whenever the tall pink figure of *Go*
stands dead center in my life, I'm off & running
before I even know why.

:Drone of the Queen Bee:

My friend in red has gone weak-kneed
over this girl in stripes. She merely points a finger
in his direction, & an excruciating joy dawns on his face.

Gone are his ever-ready quips & chortles.

As you might imagine, this has caused a rift
between Red & the rest of us.
In vague & inconsolable jealousy, my female friend

has started to show some skin. My friend in green
simply lifts the heavy boxes he is always carrying
a little higher, a kind of shrug.

My friend in blue is nowhere to be found

& won't return phone calls. Me, I'm happy
for my friend in red. I sit inside a big yellow dome
& can only wonder about the beauty of the sun's light.

:Outcasts of Infinity:

Whenever one of us gets down in the dumps,
it's up to the rest of us to come to the rescue.
The situation with Red is that he realizes

he can no longer be a drone to the Queen Bee.
My friend in blue furrows his brow
heroically. Earnest Green fashions some handcuffs

to help keep Red from working against himself
in this time of turmoil & great need. Still,
the lower half of his body disappears. We try to provide

something else for Red to focus on, all his pain
but his hope too, in danger of fading fast away.

:Hourglass Trap:

My friends & I often feel vague & listless.
There are so many things we'd like to do,
but we never seem to do anything.

Time passes us by. Time passes us by.
As each second ticks away, the mechanisms
that surround us become visible: someone

watching us on a screen, adjusting knobs to hold us in view.

2: BIG CRISIS

In Pieces

Blue arrows point to the evidence of my defeat
& my hands become hammers then shatter,
at just the barest touch, into hard streaks of light.
Under purple sky & in gathering winds, I can only change
my form so many times in one minute. First
a rocket to drag you from the dragging current

of your own worst tendencies. Current headlines
tell the whole sad story: my inevitable defeat
at the fumbling hands of my own fumbling self. First
the strange mechanical bird in the glowing sky, its shattering
cry, & then this dull but growing sense of change.
The future confuses the past. A green light

gave me permission to live in the light
of your eyes. I shift my atoms & a shocking current,
a sudden jolt, tells me what I've changed
into is not for the better. I miss you, my defeat,
my firing squad, my sweet heart-shatter.
I run a race against myself, afraid to see who'll come in first.

Dull morning: collision: aftermath. Love's first
intentions split into their constituents: separate particles of light
& the slime of want. If I could I'd shatter
your expectations, pull myself together, keep current
the lagging exchange between thought & deed. My only defeat
is my sure-fire inability to affect lasting change

in the rock face of my soul. A carved name, some spare change
that collects but doesn't ever add up. First & second
chances are more than I can ask for in this song of my lingering defeat.
I started out the hero & now I block the light
breezes that bring comfort when the mind leaves current
times behind for better. But those dreams of the past shatter

to make way for the now. I hope my now can shatter
itself, convince you of its willingness to change,
to blast forth with the zillion colors of its living current,
to worry about the beasties lurking first,
before they thrust their questioning faces into the light.
I promise an infinity of win without a single defeat,

an inner strength that can withstand the present shatter.
Prophecies tell of dawning light, then change,
a first defeat that gets swept away in the currents.

The Moon's Invisible Army

Each thought in my head is a missile,
shiny sectioned metal against
a yellow sky, & each thought thunk
is an explosion of me. For example:

the quality of mercury I love most
is that it can always scatter & re-
constitute. Boom! Or: your long arms
can turn me away or hold me close. Boom!

Living my life in the distant pink
buildings of Backgroundsville, I long
for the full-color foreground. I want
to be the first thing you look at, my face

brightly colored with any of one hundred
hundred emotions. On normal days it is blank,
a question. Cradle me in your platinum arms
& hold my head through the long & dreamless

night. I would make my body
into a sledge hammer if I could; I'd knock
each wrong thought from the sky & pound down
the door to your quietly ticking heart. Boom!

Isle of No Return

Traveling in my little metal ball, rough riveted
panels made of equal parts steel, scorn, & arrogance,

I've managed to see just about this whole big world
before deciding to call this island my home.

Protected this way, isolated, even your most devastating looks
have no effect. So go ahead & glare; those death-ray beams

turn to flower buds as they hit my chest.
Try again & though the very ground beneath my feet

catches fire & melts, I'm still standing strong.
Just what would it take for you to breach me?

The Fastest Man Alive

One note played just right
stops me in my tracks, surrounds me
with such a pleasing nimbus of white light

that I don't even want to move.
I'm riveted, rooted, waiting for what comes next
while normally, I'm gone

before I'm arrived. Normally it takes only a fraction
of a second for me to understand what
needs doing & to do it. But my speed is my doom,

a giant treadmill I seem always upon.
Every morning I wake up in the same place
I went to sleep; I can never get ahead!

I leave my problems in the dust & somehow
they meet me at the finish.
The time has come to reconsider my careen;

what good has come from bouncing away fast?
They say time is a thing that runs out,
that my buzz is nothing more than a flash.

Love Song from the Dawn of Time

Your most primal qualities turn my hands into fists,

shaggy orange hair, your sweet ape face.

A lever flips & I'm in my creature brain,

puffy red cheeks & green eyes. The real me

sits slumped in a chair & there's nothing he can do

to stop me. Lizards of the mind

breed in standing water. Every day I line up all the things

I love & give them names based on the dazzling

nature of their smiles. The mirror only shows the beast,

grunting about what he knows hurts most to hear.

Lost in the woods, there are two ways to save myself:

breathe the green of the trees & become more rooted

or scream my name & try to punch myself out.

Either way, I'm left alone

realizing that I wasn't what I wanted.

Living Whirlpool

Frantically, in the gathering dusk,
I try on one dull head after another, searching

for the proper range of responses & expressions.
Meanwhile, your colossal cold fury

dwarfs the skyline. Slowly, my arms
separate from my body & my open hands

grasp at the purpling night. I have a yellow head
for caution & a red one for those quick spats.

My cool silver head, the one that reflects,
is always just out of reach.

Your inexorable progress, your arc
of attack—I could shake the stars stunned

& still have no idea what you want from me.

I could burn down the alphabet just trying
to soothe you, this whirlpool sucking my heavy body down.

Creatures from the Past

Usually you are a sidenote, relegated
to the background, a whispered voice. Sometimes,

you're not even visible at all. In this
rocky & barren terrain of my now-head,

you don't figure in. From deep inside the forbidden cave
come creatures from the past, & you. Luckily

your memory is twenty feet tall! You keep me safe,
reminding me why we engaged

in so many experiments, why we tried to live two lives
as one through sheer alchemical persistence. Through all this,

the four arms of memory hold me tight:
good night, goodbye, good luck and good riddance.

I am happy to be reminded
of our mad scientist days. Later, after falling

through this hollow tube in my chest, I see
one of us always missed the mark.

Great Thunder!

Early morning & I'm already

cornered, thoughts scattered

like sun glint. I wish that, at least

first thing, you'd point your spears

somewhere else but your red shoes

are stunning nevertheless.

For my part, I can call down a rain of comets;

I know how to hit you where you live.

Every five minutes you think you've got me

trapped & only sometimes you're right.

You forget that I come from a future

where you can change your hair color

to match your intentions, & you can read

the instructions before you phase in.

Overhead, the grey cloud swelling with thunder

masks the sky, bright orange as the sun's light

starts to move & find its way.

Whatever you throw at me, I'm ready.

My strength comes from someplace

even I can't imagine: I have these two mystical devices

attached just below my waist.

I can walk out whenever I want.

Without A Net

One look from you & I'm someone else, turning

my back on friends, favorite foods, even my own century.

Your love is like a big stone chair, roomy

but uncomfortable. Just imagine the epic stiffness.

A golden aura around my head signals my willingness

to sell out anyone who gets in my way; the slight redness

in my eyes indicates a lack of sleep. The amount

of anger & terror I feel inside is so colossal

it will last well into the future. Robots

will have to deal with my prehistoric rage, their metal bodies

crushed by my three-clawed foot. Somewhere,

all the different aspects of myself that I used to hold dear

are trapped in clear bubbles; somewhere, each one

is getting smashed open & what comes out comes out

shivering & afraid. The sunlight turns orange.

For your love, I'd cross from one mountain to another,

walking slow on the long rope bridge to your heart

& I wouldn't turn back even if I saw you

trying to undo the knots that hold me up.

Sun Brain

Three days of bright & shiny skies & now
my mind is no longer mine own.

O burgeoning Sun Brain!
Bossed around by buoyant beams,

dictated to by a fascist, feel-good vibe,
my disposition knobs are amped up to HAPPY

& I can't stop laughing
even when you say you'd gladly steam roll me

to save yourself. Meteorologically denied my raging sadness,
I wish for a grey day; I wish my voice was confusing

rain. Eighteen beads of sweat stand out on my forehead
because I know the bullet is coming.

For ammunition I've saved up memories of faults
& failings, imagined slights. Up & down

like a rollercoaster, I can't wait for the ride to end,
one last loop around the perfect rings of Saturn

before being delivered back to the sweet
messed-up Earth. I close my eyes & let the wind

tell my hair how fast I'm moving, all my frantic
mammal concerns blowing off behind me

in the dangerously perfect light.

Human Pets

The tree uprooted. Sinister music.
Dangling, helpless, I find myself poised
for action when there is no clear warrant.

Impression is what's important;
you should be aware that, at any second,
I could pounce into the thick of things,

I could explore the unknown with such
finesse & vigor that it would gladly yield up
its most secretest of secrets to me. Let me fly

through the pale green sky of forgetfulness
& you'd better believe all those hands
that make a clumsy grab for me

will have their fingers printed. I'll know
who's taking a swipe at me.
When my errant space pod crash lands

in your new life, watch me burn
the lovely vegetation to the ground, smoke
& cinder & regret wafting.

Night time is when I get like this, always
the most challenging time for me—trying to keep it all
together when I can't even see.

Yellow beams of light projected from an object called the sun
hold me in place; ditto the look of concern on your face.
Willingly, I entered into the giant glass container

of a life with you & you alone. My torment
is that I can see out. I build a ladder one ruin
at a time, each of the one million moments

of shame & rage I feel every day
taking me higher & higher, but never over
the walls I've trapped myself behind.

Space-Boomerang Trap

What good am I if I can't put my feet on the ground?
Strapped to the giant boomerang I've made of my life,
I'm winging moonward & it's goodbye to the sweet blue

marble I've called home. Opinions challenged
turn to convictions; the clothes make the man.

Double my size & paint me golden & maybe my voice
would boom big enough to say what I mean
& what I'd say would be worth its weight. Instead

I run around & tie myself up. Against a backdrop
of white capped mountains, I kneel in front of myself

& beg forgiveness, for understanding,
for a few more minutes of sleep. If there was someone to call,
I'd call, chasing hope over the phone wires with no net

despite the cosmic pitfalls seeking to imbalance me.
A spark chases me. I go one way & then another.

Poof

So fast my fleet feet barely touch
the ground; I'm running straight out
into the nothingness of one minute I'm here,
& stern, but blink & there's just a swirl
of color where *me* used to be.
All that's left is momentum, the whispering
certainty that I at one time was.
Yesterday, I tripped coming home from the grocery
& five people circled around to gloat.
The big spotlight fell on me & left no doubt
about the source of my shame—I was center stage
& flubbing my lines, jerking my head &
arms in spastic apoplexy. "I've got the strangest feeling
I'm being turned into a puppet,"
was something I said out loud. Instantly
I had to wonder if it was my own voice
or someone else's, a hand pushed through
the hole in my back. I could feel my limbs
becoming wood, a hinge growing at my jaw.
Torn, conflicted, split down the middle, worn out
with contrarieties, questions filled my aching head:
what weatherman could have predicted this
duplicitous climate? Hoping for a thaw,
I might get sunburned. There was only one thing to do:
let everyone in on all the secrets I keep,
& do it in a big way: preempt the nightly news,
interrupt dinner, say that I sleep on my left side
exclusively & that in my dreams I go shoeless
& dream, in my dreams, of putting my feet up.

Loss Time

Sinking in the muck, I'm years

& years into the past. What

can I rely on to save me? Rain

outside & this chair becomes my throne

of doom, my one-way ticket back

to where the beasts still roam, to where

everything that should be buried

is alive & walking around.

Whenever my time sphere engulfs me,

takes me back to the way back when,

I find myself threatened, my family

& friends under attack. Once upon a time,

I was winged & shot arrows that always hit

off the mark.

Horrible Dreams

1:

Lurking, encroaching: the man
whose head I can see clear through.
Folding pink mass that sparks
with each step he takes. I'm trapped
in the air just above myself

but realize that's what's saving me.

2:

Crushing, rending: the beast
with a face like green fire, asterism
of star-bright eyes. He says he'd pull me apart
if he could, he'd grind my human sadness
to dust. He says he has no power

over those already so fractured.

3:

Lumbering, inhuman: a cybernetic
gorilla, wired & mechanical. The inexorable
jaw, a light like purpose in his eyes.
The night air is cool on the street
where I grew up. I feel safe, this most

primal protector, vigilant.

4:

Yelling, pleading: me, asleep, & me,
trying to get myself up. Just eyes & teeth.
It is day & night. My voice is not loud enough
for me to hear. The only movement
is a bird's wing which grows & grows

though nobody can see it.

5:

Jumbled, confused: an army.
Frogs who walk like men seem always to lament
the state of their souls. They want something
I have, something I didn't know I had & can't
find. There is a knock at the door, a princess

who'll sacrifice herself to save me.

6:

Released, relieved: I'm nowhere to be found.
Two men drag another man through water
again & again. "To cleanse," they say
though the man screams & scrapes to fill himself
with what's been washed away. The stars above—

I am one of them.

Tomorrow Beast

Blue sky, yellow sky, grey sky, or pale,
surface colors seep into the version of me who is
sitting here, thinking thoughts
that grow my body mountain sized,

inflating me like a balloon
set adrift in fluffy clouds.
Landmark, Point of Interest, You:
find where you're going
by using me as a reference. Then scatter;
suddenly sunderings & a quick tear.

Setting yourself up this way makes you
a target—a lighthouse that anybody with a rock
can take shots at. But I know there is tomorrow.
The Beast stomps its way
past the detritus of holdings
on & onto the vacant field of play.

We can make the same mistakes everyday,
make new ones or make none
& draw no attention to ourselves whatsoever.
Snarling, it might pass us by.

The Walls of Our Sphere

All it takes is for the right person to turn away

at just the wrong moment & the pirates start

drawing their swords & brandishing them

in a threatening & suggestive manner. The blue bird

has left my shoulder & never more will it return; ditto

the thousand colored flowers. All I ask is that you claim me

as some part of your mistaken past. Admit that there was a you

who couldn't live without me. That mountain

in the distance looks like I could climb it;

many things just don't measure up.

Monkey, lion, fox: switch places with me. Experience what it's like

for someone to look at you & not call you by your right name.

Never Be the Same Again

My life is a funhouse: giant faces taunt me
& every cornering reveals another hazard:

volcano simmering in the guest room, dinosaurs
holding bazookas. As if their teeth weren't enough,

as if your quiet rage in the next room doesn't already
split me in two. I'm stuck halfway through the wall

& there's pie on my face. The first two mirrors
show how I'd look if I were short & fat or tall & skinny,

but the third shows me as I really am: attractive,
magnetic. How else to explain the paperclips

stuck to my face, the loose change scattered over my back?
Some days I think it's better not to move at all,

to just stand & watch while the innocent tumble from the sky.
Such lovely music. Such unbelievable piercings.

The clown who runs the show didn't count on my big dumb head,
couldn't have known I'd run at high speeds into the same problems

over & over again. His red nose deflates while tears streak
the white greasepaint on his face. I can't tell you

why I do the things I do. I eat the pie off my own face,
savoring the custard of my mistakes. I run down the street

punching with both hands, knocking out
anyone who hoping to see me made a fool of.

Duel on the Island

Hidden: a meticulous list
of the many secret weapons I've stashed on my island.

Whatever the situation, I can quickly locate
my best defense. So come at me

with your giant, mutated attack whales
& I'll shrink them to tadpoles, keep them

in a glass of water & sometimes threaten
to flush them down the toilet. Drift by

on your plush & righteous flying carpet; watch
as all your pronouncements unravel in midair.

There isn't much that will surprise me.
Each medal pinned to my chest stands for a time

I got the better of somebody who tried
to get the better of me, baby.

What bothers me are the empty spots,
a different kind of badge: the misses, the failings.

Loss. In my quest to become insurmountable, to be
the strongest, the one thing no one can get past,

I've had a few set-backs. When you come at me, come quickly.
Bring any weapons you want. I'm ready.

But when you leave, leave forever. I have a feeling
& I'd rather be alone.

A Day in the Life

Any patch of land with a giant grenade buried in it

knows exactly how I feel, like I'm about to be

all up in the air. I wish my problems had names,

Colorful Costume or Dastardly Plan, but mostly

my problem is Myself. I am of two worlds, two minds,

two contradictory wardrobes, business & usual.

In the beginning, dinosaurs & sludge; years from now,

rockets to deliver me to the stiff arms of love.

But how to reconcile the various & sundry? I throw

my fear out & it always comes back. This time, I'll go instead.

Thousand-Year Separation

My room is emptying too quickly. All I have left
is a wrinkled-up rug that doesn't match anything
& now a giant green hand reaches through the wall

& grabs even that. Who can see the humongous question mark
that hangs over my head & who can read the small
blurry script inside? I want to know where it's all gone

& how to get it back. But I'm wrestling with myself,
with the future of what I didn't know I had & now
can't live without. A quick minute is too long to live like this.

My hands are bound in spangled silver & I can't even wave
goodbye. All the junk that surrounds me
is junk I don't want: spare change, wax lips, rotten fruit.

Sure, I can excite my molecules one at a time
by remembering my happiest moments;
I can vibrate right out of my skin with past joy, but

It's an empty hand waving in the air. I still have these questions:
what about the candlelight that burns in the day
& what about the green sphere bouncing around my head

singing "Go!" Why am I the same month after month
—persecuted, split, empty & failed?
Will I ever be able to hold my sad tired head in my hands?

Requiem for the End of Time!

Assume there's someone else

pulling my strings, my mouth

opening to say the one thing

that will bring you back to me

but uttering nonsense instead.

Covered with cloud, I'm shaking

as my stupidity grows to silly

proportions. Yesterday morning

I saw the hooded man with the axe, yes,

I was led onto the stage & told to sing

my last. I inhaled & what I inhaled

turned me into a robot, my limbs

clunky & hollow, my chest filled

with gears & pistons where

breathing & love used to be.

I have a glowing faith

that eventually I will leave all this in the past.

In the Hot Seat

Orange & pink flames spurt from my head
when I see your small figure approaching this structure
I'm shackled to. But all your gizmos & contraptions
won't save you from the new fury I've learned.
Helicopters circle & report on the duel we've begun;
the tail end of your streaky & strained hopes

wraps around my heart fifteen times & my hopes
& my dreams & my fears & the ensuing light staggers mine empty head
into filling itself with itself. Once I've begun
down any path, I won't turn back. I lack structure
which is a way of saying I've never learned how
to live without you: saggy-heart you, you love contraption.

I hold up my big dumb hand to redirect your conniptions,
I grow spikes on my softest parts in hopes
you'll find another flower to land on. Quickly I learn
you won't be denied your just piece of my hide & my head.
It's the least I owe you for the trouble I've caused. A complex structure
of grief cracks its crystalline supports under the strain of our *once begun,*

now ending debacle. Only after can anyone say they'd begun
with the best intentions, implication itself such a sorry contraption,
a broken-down engine for communicating the structure
of this when you said that. My wrists chafe at the ropes
that hold me back, my own inabilities like robots, metal-headed
& clunking emptily with preprogrammed codes pre-learned,

ready to execute, ready to self-destruct. What is there to learn
from aftermath, from a survey of where this began?
Sleep in volcanoes & you risk getting blown out of your head;
roll over my foot in your rickety contraption
& watch me walk off as the pale sunset burns off thin hope.
There is an inherent difference in our processes, the very structure

of our sorrow. Anger & fear balanced with regret sutured
to a never-ending sense of having given up on the learning curve.
You end up somewhere better than you started, a buzzing hope
that the bees who make your honey will finish what they've begun,
that love plus love can build a lasting machine, a souped-up contraption
to get its occupants safely out of their own heads

& into some gleaming hope mobile, some holy holy structure.
When you begin to ascend those divine stairs, your head
clears, you learn to become a better pilot of the contraption you've got.

3: THE BRAVE & THE BOLD

Well, they are gone, and here must I remain...

—Samuel Taylor Coleridge,
"This Lime-Tree Bower My Prison"

:The Hole in the Sky:

Walking home when the sky was blue-night purple,
Red noticed & directed our attention to a hole
opening. "Look!" was what he said
to get us to share his startled & uncertain perception
of the hole opening up in the sky.

Suddenly, long yellow tentacles dropped from the hole
& wrapped around us. They pulled us into the sky,
closer & closer to the hole that floated in the purple
blue-night vastness. I considered the question of perception
& wondered aloud: "This might be a good thing," I said.

:Forbidden:

Sometimes my friends & I, we get to feeling persecuted.
You see, we have a strong sense of entitlement
& deep stores of confidence that we are, individually

& collectively, the most awesomest thing of all time.
You can see us holding signs on street corners
demanding equal rights, better treatment, final aesthetic control.

We deal with the overwhelming apathy that the public
shows to our cause by looking sullen for days on end.
Then we go back to seeking out people to strut our stuff

in front of, bragging in our every action how utterly cool
we are. When this goes unrecognized, we get mean.
Everyone should realize they are nothing compared to us.

:Sensational Spectacular:

When my friends & I sit at the same table
we all get to thinking that our actions are the important ones,

the ones that define the times we live in & that, logically,
we are the most important people alive right now

& that our thoughts are more colorful & exotic & sweeping
than anyone else's. Then a lightning bolt

strikes the table & cuts it jaggedly in two,
our resulting fear the most spectacular & sensational fear ever expressed.

:The Most Dangerous Earth of All:

On account of his earnest & up-standing nature,
his do-good intentions, Green often finds he is
at war with himself. He described it to me once:

"It is like I have two brains in my head, one that tells me
to build a bridge that helps orphans get the medical treatment
they need & one that tells me just blow up the whole city
my ex-girlfriend lives in." Times like this, my friend Green
freaks me out a little bit. He says, "We are living
on the most dangerous Earth of all!" & then pulls his fist back

to hit himself square in his own square jaw.
Uncertain of the outcome, I always leave him to himself,
hopeful that we'll end up on a safer Earth someday.

:Runaway Room:

What I hate is when my friends & I
are all having a serious conversation

about appropriately serious subjects
when—out of nowhere—the floor of the room

rips itself out of the building & hurtles
into orbit above the Earth,

creating too vast a distance for us to bridge.

:Hedging:

Because of our recent difficulties,
my friends & I have explored the possibility
of renting a house somewhere together,
somewhere we can be on our own & undisturbed,
& not have to worry about break away rooms.

The rental agent had the kind of eyes that pierce
into the very soul. He said, "I have a warehouse
you may find suitable." But when we quibbled
over the price (too high for us, simple friends
wanting to spend time together), he looked at us

& made us ashamed we hadn't offered all we could.

:World's Finest:

Green & Red are always getting into fights,
with each other as well as with anything
that gets in their paths. They're the first
to get into trouble. Their actions land them
in hot water more often than you might think.

My blue friend has to fly in to save them every time.

It might be natural for Red & Green to grow resentful
of Blue, who is always having to bail them out.
Instead, they seem grateful that he's around
to break people's arms, to deflect thrown rocks,
to poke out the eyes in the giant green face that giggles

at us all when we mess up. Blue, however, thinks about
leaving their skinny asses in a sling one of these days.

:Deadly Dreams:

Each of my friends has crazy-whack dreams:

Green dreams himself into a field,
one hundred thousand blades of grass relying on him;

Red dreams he is a fish;

my female friend dreams of flying free
through the air, no visible plane to separate her from sky;

Blue claims his dreams are completely realistic,
& offer him neither release or solace;

my dream is of a giant gladiator, fist cocked
to knock me into next week but who never moves,

a constant threat to keep me in line.

:Battle Against the Bodiless Uniform:

After one tiring day of doing nothing with my friends,
I came home, threw my clothes onto the bed

& got right into the shower. After I got out,
I saw what looked like me lying in bed already:

my clothes laid out exactly as if I was in them!
I took advantage of this rare chance to tell myself a thing or two.

:Who This Monster Really Is:

Grey clawed hands swinging hurdy-gurdy,
this blue-crested monster barges in on me & my friends
making all kinds of ridiculous demands:
cover the driveway with lollipop wrappers,
pluck unruly blades of grass from the front lawn

with only your teeth. We're all uncertain
of how to respond, hoping for some kind of reprieve.
My friend in blue suddenly can't see; Red feels
like his legs are stuck together. All of us
seem literally disabled in the face of one

who demands impossible demands be met.

:Where Are All My Friends?:

In the scariest part of the night, a storm kicks up—
pink, yellow, & pale aqua colored lightning
streaks up the whole sky & tiny hailstones,

each the size of new fears, strike the window glass.
"I'd sooner die than call anyone & admit my terror,"
I say clearly to myself, hoping the phone will ring.

:Knock-Out:

Yesterday, my friend in blue took a right hook to the jaw,
sat down depressed on the school yard, & just looked
at the rest of us. His eyes told of the pity of deserts,

the yawning emptiness of marshmallows. Since then,
he hasn't talked to us, our sad protector. Seen just now
with some people who were not any of us, my other friends & I

worry we'll have to start defending ourselves
& turn our highest degree of vigilance inward.

:Irresistible Force:

Blue called last night to say he was doing well
& how are we all doing & is it ok if he comes by
to pick up those cds he let me borrow because, frankly,
he's doing so great he doesn't think he'll ever need
to call us "friends" again.
                                Come by in the afternoon,
I say, wondering how any car radio could ever be turned
so loud that could hear it from the street: two floors up
sitting in the back bedroom closet with the door shut tight.

:Free For All:

Since Blue has decided he wants out, the rest of us
have subtly turned on each other. Red & Green,
always uncomfortable around each other,
have started actively sabotaging the hopes of the other.

Red has written numerous letters
to a popular Hollywood actress, letting her know
that Green is dangerous when bereft of his blankie,
that he likes to eat cow dung.

Green secretly changed Red's mailing address
so that Red will always walk back lonely from the mailbox.

My female friend thinks these are the end times,
that the starfish who loses a limb won't grow it back,
but instead will devour the others
out of a misguided sense of symmetry.

:Immovable Object:

For reasons beyond anyone's control, our female friend
has taken a job in a different city & will soon move
far far away. No attempt is made to contact Blue.
Red & Green have already begun talking about how
they really missed out by never expressing their true feelings
to our mutual female friend & their love
inflates in retrospect.

:Try-Outs:

My remaining two friends & I hold a one-day try-out
in an effort to bolster our diminishing ranks.

Just before the end of the day, we get our only four applicants.

Each has so many problems that the score sheets
Green drew up don't help us much. At the end,

the four we turned down go off together, their happinesses
outnumbering ours by one.

:Spin-Off:

Green & Red have begun talking about getting an apartment
in the city. We joke about the vision of the two of them

with a masking tape line down the center of their apartment
dividing all the space & stuff between the two of them.

When I close my eyes, I see my own home divided,
one side for all the things I can handle & the other for things I can't.

:King-Size:

This morning, I felt too big for my own feet.

:Super Struggle:

After weeks of fighting it, I admit that this is the end
of us friends. In the night, a big hulking man comes to me
& hammers my head repeatedly with a stoplight that he held

daintily between giant thumb & giant forefinger. Green & Red
have stopped speaking to each other, a silence that will last,
by definition, until one of them makes a sound.

:Thud!:

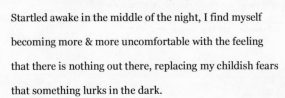

Startled awake in the middle of the night, I find myself

becoming more & more uncomfortable with the feeling

that there is nothing out there, replacing my childish fears

that something lurks in the dark.